OCT 09 '01

Oprah Winfrey

An Unauthorized Biography

Gini Holland

Heinemann Library
Chicago, Illinois

© 2001 Reed Educational & Professional Publishing
Published by Heinemann Library,
an imprint of Reed Educational & Professional Publishing,
Chicago, IL

Customer Service 888-454-2279

Visit our website at www.heinemannlibrary.com

Produced for Heinemann Library by Discovery Books
Designed by Ian Winton
Originated by Dot Gradations
Printed and bound in Hong Kong/China

Library of Congress Cataloging-in-Publication Data
Holland, Gini.
    Oprah Winfrey / Gini Holland.
        p. cm. – (Heinemann profiles)
    Includes bibliographical references and index.
    ISBN 1-58810-061-8 (library binding)
    1. Winfrey, Oprah—Juvenile literature. 2. Television personalities—United
States—Biography—Juvenile literature. 3. Motion picture actors and actresses—United
States—Biography—Juvenile literature. [1. Winfrey, Oprah. 2. Television personalities. 3.
Actors and actresses. 4. Afro-Americans—Biography. 5. Women—Biography.] I. Title. II.
Series.

PN1992.4.W56 H65 2001
791.45'028'092—dc21
[B]   00-047225

Acknowledgments
The Publishers would like to thank the following for permission to reproduce photographs:
Popperfoto, pp. 5, 9, 33, 35, 37; Corbis, pp. 7, 10, 11, 12, 17, 20, 21, 26, 31, 32, 39; Gini Holland,
pp. 14, 15; Aquarius, pp. 23, 29, 40; Rex Features, pp. 28, 30, 42, 45, 47, 48, 51; Topham Picture
Point, p. 34.

Cover photograph reproduced with permission of Popperfoto

Every effort has been made to contact copyright holders of any material reproduced in this book.
Any omissions will be rectified in subsequent printings if notice is given to the publisher.

Some words are shown in bold, **like this.** You can find out what they mean by looking in
the glossary.

This is an unauthorized biography. The subject has not sponsored or endorsed this book.

CONTENTS

WHO IS OPRAH WINFREY?

There are many talk-show hosts on television, but there is only one Oprah. Her unique style is copied by many people, from interviewers to politicians. But none have been able to match either her popularity or her income. *The Oprah Winfrey Show* is broadcast to 132 countries worldwide. Oprah's combined talents and business sense will soon make her the nation's first African-American billionaire. Her show has received more than 30 Emmys and many other awards for achievement.

Some blame Oprah for turning daytime television into a string of shows about social misfits and terrible relationships. In spite of this criticism, she is one of the country's most beloved celebrities—and

Being famous

Fame is a major factor in Oprah's daily life, but at first it took her by surprise. She once said, "I was walking down the street the other day, and a woman bus driver pulled her bus over, jumped off it, and ran down the street to shake my hand. The bus was full, and this was five o'clock traffic, but the passengers loved it. Everyone was clapping, and I said to myself, 'This is something. I must be a somebody!'"

one of its most influential people. In the United States, more than twenty million viewers a week watch her show. Oprah also has a website packed with topics of interest for her audience. Her new magazine, O, puts her point of view on the newsstands. Harpo, her **production company,** produces movies for television and film. Whether these shows star Oprah herself or other actors, they are stamped with her values and ideas.

In 1988, Oprah received the People's Choice Award for Broadcaster of the Year.

MOST TRUSTED

What is Oprah's secret to success? She is possibly the most trusted woman in the United States. Her fans trust her to entertain, inspire, educate, and understand. They trust her to accept them just as they are, even when she challenges them to be better. At the same time, many people think of Oprah Winfrey as a television version of their favorite next-door neighbor. In fact, most of her fans are not in awe of her—they just want to invite her over for coffee.

EARLY YEARS IN CHANGING TIMES

Oprah Winfrey was born on January 29, 1954, to unwed teenage parents, in Kosciusko, Mississippi, one of the poorest areas of the country. Her parents named her after the biblical character Orpah, but her name was misspelled as Oprah on her birth certificate. No one ever corrected the mistake. When Oprah was still a baby, her mother, Vernita Lee, left her to be raised by her grandparents.

At her grandparents' farm, Oprah was poor and lonely: "The nearest neighbor was a blind man up the road. There weren't other kids—no playmates, no toys except for the one **corncob doll.** I played with the animals and made speeches to the cows."

SPEAKING FROM EXPERIENCE

Oprah lived in terror of her grandfather, who often tried to shoo her away from him with his cane. Her grandmother beat Oprah when she misbehaved. She told Oprah that she was doing it for her own good, because she loved her. "I still don't think that was love," says Oprah now. As an adult, Oprah has often spoken out against child abuse. She says that it is partly to blame for many of society's problems because of the message of violence and a lack of understanding that it sends to young people.

"Oprah's law"

In 1991, Oprah testified before the U.S. Senate on behalf of the National Child Protection Act that she herself had initiated. This resulted in a national law that requires that all convicted child abusers be listed on a national database. Known to many as the "Oprah bill" or "Oprah's law," it was signed into law by President Bill Clinton on December 20, 1993.

Oprah Winfrey spoke at the inauguration of President Bill Clinton on January 17, 1993.

LOVE OF LEARNING

Oprah's grandmother taught her to read by the time she was three. When Oprah started kindergarten at the age of five, she was bored. But even then, Oprah was good at speaking up for herself. She wrote her teacher a note that said, "Dear Miss New. I don't think I belong here." Impressed with Oprah's skills, Miss New moved her up to first grade.

> "Reading gave me hope. For me it was the open door."
> Oprah Winfrey, 1997

Bigger changes lay ahead. Around 1960, Oprah moved north to Milwaukee, Wisconsin, to live with her mother. Oprah had to get used to living in a city instead of the country, and to living with a parent she barely knew. She did not feel at home or even very welcome there. Oprah has explained, "I felt like I was an outcast. I don't know why mother ever decided she wanted me. She wasn't equipped to take care of me. I was just an extra burden to her." Oprah's half-sister, Patricia, had lighter skin, which Oprah thought made her prettier. So Oprah decided to take comfort in being the smarter of the two.

At the end of first grade, Oprah moved south again, this time to Nashville, Tennessee, to live with her father, Vernon Winfrey. Once again, teachers recognized her ability and moved her up, this time to third grade. Then she returned to live with her

mother in Milwaukee. Despite being shuffled between parents, Oprah did well in school and learned how to work hard to get ahead: "I felt it happen in the fourth grade. Something came over me. I turned in a book report early and it got such a good response, I thought, 'I'm gonna do that again.'"

LEARNING DIFFERENT RULES

Moving between two parents showed Oprah the difference that parents' expectations and limits can make. She has explained, "Growing up, I acted differently when being raised by my mother than being raised by my father. I would break **curfew.** I'd stay out. I'd run the streets. Because I knew I could get away with it . . . On the other hand, my father didn't even have to say it. You just knew. . . ."

SEGREGATION AND POVERTY

During the 1950s in the United States, African Americans could be legally **segregated** from white society. In many places, they could not go to whites-only schools. African-American-only schools had less money for teachers, books, buildings, and even heating than white schools did. Today, African Americans, who make up thirteen percent of the country's population, are still a minority in the United States. However, Americans of all races, including African Americans, now have the same **civil rights.**

In the north, many landlords sought to prevent African Americans from living in good neighborhoods. Discrimination kept them from getting good jobs. Oprah, like many African Americans then, lived in poverty. She remembers life

During Oprah's early childhood, segregation laws kept African Americans from attending white-only schools. These people are demonstrating against ending segregation.

in Milwaukee: "We were so poor we couldn't afford a dog or cat, so I made pets out of two cockroaches. . . You wanted pets, all you had to do was go in the kitchen at night and turn on the lights. You could find a whole family of them. So I would name them and put them in a jar and feed them. . . I called them things like 'Melinda' and 'Sandy.'"

FIGHTING FOR POLITICAL POWER

In most of the **rural** south, African Americans were denied the right to vote until the civil rights movement began during the 1960s. They had neither political power nor representation. There were no African-American mayors, sheriffs, or senators to look out for their interests.

African-American workers were often hired last and fired first. They were almost always paid less than white workers. With no power and little money or education, many African-American families were at the bottom of the social and economic ladder. Unfortunately, at the time, many white people wanted them to stay there.

THE BIRTH OF CIVIL RIGHTS

In 1954, the year Oprah was born, the U.S. Supreme Court first ruled that **segregation** was neither fair nor legal. The case was *Brown v. Board of Education*. The parents of Linda Brown, a seven-year-old African-American girl, successfully **sued** the Topeka, Kansas, school board to allow their daughter to attend her local, whites-only school. This case ended legal school segregation in the United States.

The following year, on December 1, 1955, an African-American woman named Rosa Parks

Rosa Parks's protest against bus segregation in Alabama paved the way for progress in the fight for civil rights.

refused to give up her bus seat to a white man in Montgomery, Alabama. She was arrested and fined for violating segregation laws.

African Americans in Montgomery sought the help of the **civil rights** leader Dr. Martin Luther King Jr., and they organized a year-long **boycott** of the buses. Eventually, the Supreme Court declared bus segregation laws illegal. By the end of 1955, schools and public transportation were for the first time fully open to African Americans. Rosa Parks has been called "the mother of the civil rights movement." Her simple act of courage led to one of the first successes of non-violent protest for civil rights.

THE GOAL OF CIVIL RIGHTS

During the late 1950s and throughout the 1960s, the civil rights movement worked hard to change the country's policy from segregation to **integration.** The goal was to have people of all races and religions live in harmony, share equal civil rights, and have equal opportunities.

But, in the very beginning, integration caused some unexpected problems for African Americans. Oprah herself was to learn that lesson when integration provided her with a new educational opportunity.

Integrating Two Worlds

Moving backward and forward between relatives, Oprah learned to adapt to changing rules and expectations. However, what was perhaps her biggest challenge came in high school.

Freed from segregation

It was one of Oprah's teachers, Eugene A. Abrams, who made it happen. Around 1966, Oprah was enrolled at Lincoln High School in Milwaukee, where 99 percent of the students were African Americans. The classes were overcrowded, and the building was run down. Most students were from poor, uneducated families. It was hard for students to work well in such an environment.

Mr. Abrams was surprised one day to find Oprah reading a book during lunch. Realizing what a serious student Oprah was, Abrams helped her get a **scholarship** to Nicolet, an all-white, well-respected high school in the wealthy **suburb** of Fox Point.

Until 1967, Oprah went to Lincoln High School in Milwaukee. Conditions in inner-city schools at the time made learning difficult.

Oprah, shown here in her school yearbook for 1966–1967, took her studies seriously.

COOL TO BE BLACK

The growing **civil rights** movement convinced many Americans that **integration** was the right thing to do. Oprah remembers, "It was the first time that I was exposed to the fact that I was not like all the other kids. In 1968 it was real hip to know a black person, so I was very popular." This situation made Oprah uneasy: "The kids would all bring me back to their houses, bring out their maid from the back, and say, 'Oprah, do you know Mabel?' They figured all blacks knew each other. It was real strange and real tough."

RICH FRIENDS, POOR FAMILY

The 18-mile (30-kilometer) bus ride home from Fox Point to the inner city was like commuting between different planets. Oprah has said, "The life that I saw those children lead was so totally different than what I went home to. I wanted my mother to be like their mothers. . . . But her way of showing love to me was getting out and going to work every day, putting clothes on my back, and having food on the table. At that time I didn't understand it."

Oprah Changes Course

The stress of living in two worlds—one rich, one poor—was often too much for Oprah. Plus, she had other problems with family and friends. She began to disobey her mother and get into trouble. Oprah even tried to steal $200 from her mother to run away. Vernita finally threatened to put Oprah in a home for troubled teenagers. But when the home could not take her immediately, Vernita called Oprah's father, who brought her back to live with him and his wife in Nashville.

Saved by her father

Oprah is grateful that her father was strict. "When my father took me, it changed the course of my life. He saved me. He simply knew what he wanted and expected. He would take nothing less," she said.

"My father turned my life around by making me see that being your best was the best you could be. His love of learning showed me the way....I have a great father who used to tell me, 'Listen, girl, if I tell you a mosquito can pull a wagon, don't ask me no questions. Just hitch him up.'"
Oprah Winfrey, 1997

Vernon Winfrey set a firm dress code for Oprah. He would not let her wear halter tops or tight, short skirts. He wanted her to look and behave like a proper young woman. He demanded excellence in her schoolwork as well.

ROLE MODELS FROM HISTORY

Because Oprah read so much, many of her **role models** came from history. One of the first speeches Oprah memorized, Sojourner Truth's powerful

"Ain't I a Woman?" speech, is still one of her favorites. Truth was a **slave** who, after a long struggle to win her own freedom, spoke at the Women's Rights Convention in Akron, Ohio, in 1851. She said, "That man over there says that a woman needs to be helped into carriages and lifted over ditches and have the best place everywhere. Nobody ever helps me into carriages or over mud puddles or gives me any best place and ain't I a woman?…"

FIRST SUCCESSES

In her father's home, Oprah began to thrive. One of the first African Americans to attend East Nashville High School, Oprah was voted "Most Popular Girl." This time she could cope with, and enjoy, the attention. Vernon drove her to speech competitions all over the state. This experience turned out to be very beneficial to her career.

Oprah became an **honors student,** and her hard work began to pay off in both travel and awards. When she was seventeen, Oprah was invited to President Richard M. Nixon's White House

Early tragedy

Instead of becoming one of the world's most famous entertainers, Oprah Winfrey could have become an unmarried teenage mother. At the age of fourteen, after a pregnancy of only six months, Oprah gave birth to a baby boy. The baby died shortly afterward. Years later, when her half-sister told national magazines this family secret, Oprah turned a negative situation into a positive one by discussing it on her show. Oprah has made a point of discussing the problems of teens, the causes of teen pregnancy, and the tough choices some teens have to make.

Conference on Youth in Estes Park, Colorado. She competed for the title of "Outstanding Teenager of America." After winning first place in the National Forensic League Tournament in Tennessee, a contest for speakers and debaters, Oprah unsuccessfully competed against other winners in the final at Stanford University in Palo Alto, California.

VOLUNTEERING LEADS TO RADIO

In 1971, while Oprah was still in high school, her speaking abilities and personality led to her first job in broadcasting. Disc jockey John Heidelberg noticed Oprah when she asked him to sponsor her in a charity walk. "I admired her voice," he explained later. "She was articulate." After persuading Vernon to let her take the job, Oprah began to train after school and on weekends at the local radio station, WVOL. Soon she was reading the news for $100 a week. This job was the start of an amazing media career.

Technical tips

- John Heidelberg taught Oprah techniques such as how to speak into a microphone
- without hissing her s's or popping her p's, as well as to never turn her head away from the
- microphone when speaking.

COLLEGE AND CROWNS

After high school, Oprah attended college at Tennessee State University. However, her developing career would mean that it was many years before she would graduate. Many young people cannot afford the expense of college, but Oprah found a way. She competed in beauty pageants, where her talents in acting often helped her win. Beauty contests helped Oprah pay her tuition fees and polish her stage skills. Best of all, they also brought exciting travel opportunities.

In March 1972, Oprah was crowned Miss Black Nashville. She then went on to win Miss Black

Contestants pose during an African-American beauty contest in the 1970s. Prize money from beauty contests paid for Oprah's college tuition.

Tennessee. Oprah has said, "I won on poise and talent. I was raised to believe that the lighter your skin, the better you were. I wasn't light-skinned, so I decided to be the best and the smartest." As Miss Black Tennessee, Oprah won a **scholarship** and an an all-expenses-paid trip to Hollywood for the Miss Black America pageant.

Stars leave their handprints in this Hollywood sidewalk. Becoming a star was Oprah's childhood dream.

Going to Hollywood and becoming a star was a childhood dream for Oprah. She did not win the Miss Black America crown, but she touched the names of stars written in the pavement outside Mann's Chinese Theater in Hollywood. Oprah just knew her name would be there some day. To make her dream come true, she decided to study speech and drama in college.

BLACK PRIDE, OPRAH-STYLE

Unlike many African Americans at that time, Oprah did not demonstrate in Black Pride activities. She took a different path. She worked to overcome **stereotypes,** to do things that had previously been considered for whites only—and often for white *men* only.

Oprah's desire to become a **newscaster** and TV interviewer was partly inspired by her admiration for Barbara Walters. When Oprah was growing up,

"People see me and they see that I am black, that's something that I celebrate. But I don't feel that it's something that I need to wave a banner about, which used to cause me all kinds of problems in college. I was not a dashiki-wearing kind of woman."

Oprah Winfrey, 1987

few women of any color were on television in serious roles. Barbara Walters was the first—and only—television news woman in the U.S. during the 1960s. Walters has a way of gaining people's trust so that she can ask personal questions and get good answers. "I thank God for Barbara Walters," Oprah has said. "She's a **pioneer** and she paved the way for the rest of us."

Award-winning journalist Barbara Walters was a source of inspiration to Oprah, the young, aspiring newscaster.

Role model

Barbara Walters is acknowledged worldwide as one of television's most respected interviewers and **journalists.** In 1976, Walters became the first woman to co-host a national news show. Her career highlights include an interview with President Fidel Castro of Cuba and a joint interview with former Egyptian president Anwar Sadat and Menachem Begin, the former prime minister of Israel. She also has interviewed every U.S. president since Richard M. Nixon.

Leaping from Radio to Television

In 1973, Oprah made her important career move from radio to TV. Still in her **sophomore year** of college, Oprah became the first African-American **news anchor** at Nashville's WTVF-TV. She was also the first female co-anchor in the city's history.

Helped by changing times

Before the 1960s, television hired only white men as **newscasters** and talk-show hosts. Some people said that the African Americans and women who were hired in the 1960s were just there to show that news stations practiced **integration.** But Oprah did not mind. She felt it gave the opportunity to show what an African-American woman could do, given the chance. As she put it, "I was a **token,** but I was a happy, paid token." She was also extremely talented. Chris Clark, of Nashville's WTVF-TV, described Oprah's audition tape: "It was unbelievable. You looked at Oprah the first time and you said, 'This is right. This will work.' It was just one of those things you don't experience very often."

Challenges in Baltimore

Oprah's next job took her to the east coast—to Baltimore, Maryland, in 1976, where she became co-anchor of the 6 P.M. news with Jerry Turner. Turner expected a polished, professional **journalist** at his side, but instead he got Oprah, who broke down and cried on the air as she covered one particularly heartbreaking story.

> "It was not good for a news reporter to be out covering a fire and crying with a woman who has lost her home. It was very hard for me to all of a sudden become 'Ms. Broadcast Journalist' and not feel things."
>
> Oprah Winfrey, 1994

As Oprah has explained, "I was twenty-two years old. I had no business anchoring the news in a major market. Sitting down with the god of local anchormen intimidated me." On April 1, 1977, she was pulled from the news show. The station then attempted to remake her image. The assistant news director said that "her eyes were too wide apart, her nose was too flat and broad, her chin was too big, and her hair was too thick and a complete mess." But however they tried to change her appearance, Oprah's unique reporting style was already in place. She might not have looked like a typical news anchor, but her genuineness and her clear, midwest accent appealed to a wide audience.

LESSONS AND FRIENDSHIP

As she worked with image makers, Oprah learned when to listen. She also learned when to say "no" to other people's ideas of how she should present herself. She learned to do news interviews, and how to **network** with people in the business. Baltimore provided an excellent training ground for Oprah to become a star.

NETWORKING AND RATINGS

In 1977, Oprah was asked to co-host a local morning talk show called *People Are Talking*. Oprah really listened to her audience, and this allowed her

Oprah, shown here in 1986, proved people wrong when they said the talk show formula was on its way out.

to ask great follow-up questions. Soon the Baltimore **ratings** showed her beating a nationally broadcast talk show hosted by the extremely popular Phil Donahue. This was an astonishing feat.

Sherry Burns, the **producer** of *People Are Talking,* recognized Oprah's natural abilities and looks. "She's the universal woman," Burns said. "She's a totally approachable, real, warm person. Who she is on camera is exactly what she is off camera…. She was and is *the* communicator." Assistant producer Debra DiMaio said, "Her stamina was boggling."

Debra DiMaio helped Oprah land her big break hosting *AM Chicago.* When DiMaio moved to a Chicago TV production job, she showed one of Oprah's *People Are Talking* tapes to station manager Dennis Swanson. Swanson said, "That young woman was sensational. I brought in all my program people, and they agreed. So I called her. When you've looked at as many audition tapes as I have, [ones like] hers just jumped out of the stack."

Oprah's best friend, Gayle King Bumpas, was the only person who supported Oprah's move to Chicago: "Everybody, with the exception of my best friend, told me it wouldn't work. They said I was black, female, and overweight…and the talk show **formula** was on its way out."

SWEET HOME CHICAGO

In January 1984, when Oprah began to host *AM Chicago*, she jumped into a huge television market. By 1986, this local TV talk show, which was now called *The Oprah Winfrey Show,* was airing nationally. More importantly, it was competing well with New York-based *The Phil Donahue Show.* Oprah's popularity surprised even her friends. Oprah explains, "Chicago is one of the most racially **volatile** cities anywhere. Our success there shows that race ...can be **transcended**."

Oprah, a successful talk show host, wanted to be taken seriously as an actress, too.

A NIGHT AT THE OSCARS

By day, Oprah worked on her show. But she had other projects to work on after hours. In 1985, determined to prove herself as a serious actress, she negotiated a role in the film version of Alice Walker's novel, *The Color Purple*. To film in Hollywood and South Carolina for almost three months, Oprah had to take time off from her television show. Guest hosts and reruns of old shows aired during her absence, but her fans remained loyal. In her role as Sofia, Oprah expressed the difficulties faced by African-American women. Oprah said Sofia "represents a legacy of black women and the bridges that I've crossed over to get where I am." Oprah was nominated for an **Oscar** for Best Supporting Actress for her role.

Oprah, who played Sofia in *The Color Purple*, is known for her roles as strong women who overcome terrible difficulties.

SIDE PROJECTS GALORE

There seems to be no end to Oprah's projects, large and small. In 1986, with the help of her staff, Oprah formed a Big Sister group for two dozen girls. These girls lived in one of the worst **housing projects** in Chicago. Oprah met and talked to them. She later said, "When we talk about goals, and they say they want Cadillacs, I say, 'If you cannot talk correct[ly], if you cannot read or do math, if you become pregnant, if you drop out of school, you will never have a Cadillac, I guarantee it!'" The following year Oprah found time to finish her studies so that she could graduate from Tennessee State University.

Oprah donates millions of dollars to charity, in particular to boys' and girls' clubs, high schools, and colleges that serve African Americans.

In 1997, after the deaths of Mother Teresa and Princess Diana, Oprah founded the Angel Network to continue their charitable work. The Angel Network programs began with "Build an Oprah House," in partnership with Habitat for Humanity, a worldwide home-building program. Oprah's TV pleas for support sparked a huge increase in volunteers and donations for the cause. The Angel Network also started "The World's Largest Piggy Bank," in which people donate their spare change to a **scholarship** fund for poor children.

Oprah performs for participants of the 1995 Mother's Day 5K Walk in Central Park.

Oprah has also set up other charities, including the Family for Better Lives Foundation.

Oprah has donated millions of dollars to charity. She has given her **alma mater,** Tennessee State University, large donations. She has given millions to colleges that serve African-American men and women and to Chicago-area high schools and boys' and girls' clubs. Since Oprah located her company, Harpo Studios, in West Chicago, a degree of prosperity has started to return to a run-down part of the city.

"Her public life is very well known. Her private life is very private. I shall only tell you this of her private life: almost any time you read that some anonymous donor has given a great gift to a body of students—black students, white students, Asian, Spanish-speaking, Native American, Aleut—when you see 'anonymous,' whisper to yourself, 'Oprah'."
                    Dr. Maya Angelou, introducing Oprah as guest
                              speaker at Salem College in May 2000

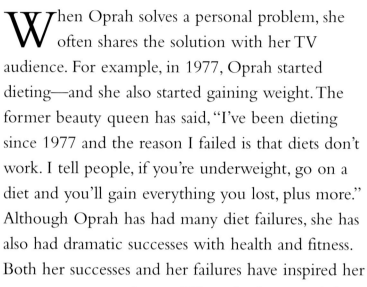

FACING PERSONAL PROBLEMS

When Oprah solves a personal problem, she often shares the solution with her TV audience. For example, in 1977, Oprah started dieting—and she also started gaining weight. The former beauty queen has said, "I've been dieting since 1977 and the reason I failed is that diets don't work. I tell people, if you're underweight, go on a diet and you'll gain everything you lost, plus more." Although Oprah has had many diet failures, she has also had dramatic successes with health and fitness. Both her successes and her failures have inspired her viewers. When she is overweight, her fans think, "She's got problems just like the rest of us. If she can be successful in life, so can I." On the other hand, when Oprah looks healthy and slim, her viewers think, "If Oprah can solve a personal problem like that, so can I."

Oprah has one advantage over most people who are trying to lose weight—she can afford to hire people to help her get in shape. To help solve her weight problem, Oprah hired chef Rosie Daley to help her improve her eating habits.

By 1996, Oprah's dieting had paid off. Since then, she has explored issues of weight and fitness on many of her shows.

Then she and Rosie co-wrote a diet book called *In the Kitchen with Rosie*. The book became a best-seller, and so did *Make the Connection*, an exercise and fitness book Oprah co-wrote with fitness trainer Bob Greene. Oprah freely admits she loves greasy junk food as much as healthful meals, but her more serious problem was her habit of **binge eating.** She has explored these issues on many of her shows. Weight and fitness continue to be major concerns for Oprah and for many of her television viewers.

FACING ABUSE

Sometimes Oprah's show forces her to face problems from her childhood. When Oprah was nine, a male relative began to touch her in ways that were inappropriate. She was young and afraid to tell her mother at the time, but much later she raised the subject of the sexual abuse of children on one of her shows. In sharing her experience on national television, Oprah discovered that she was not alone. This helped her to understand her feelings better.

Generous Oprah

Even after becoming rich and famous, Oprah never forgot her family. She bought homes for her mother, her father and stepmother, and for her half-sister. Her cousin Jo Baldwin, Vice President of Harpo, told *Ebony* magazine, "Oprah is generous to a fault."

POVERTY AND THE PAST

Poverty is another dark side of Oprah's past. Her father owned businesses such as a neighborhood barbershop and a grocery store. This allowed him to give her a middle-class life.

However, when Oprah lived in Milwaukee, her mother's job took care of only the bare necessities. Now that Oprah is one of the wealthiest women in the world, she has to think carefully about how to help her relatives. She believes she has to balance her generosity with encouragement for them to help themselves. Even so, some family members have complained that she does not do enough for them.

Now that she is wealthy, she is also a tempting target for lawsuits. So Oprah has to watch what she says.

After Oprah's April 1996 show about **mad cow disease,** Texas cattle farmers worried that her fans would stop eating hamburger meat. So they tried to **sue** her

Oprah enters court with her defense lawyers during the Texas trial in January 1998. As one of the world's most influential women, anything Oprah says carries weight.

• •

for comments she had made about beef. Oprah went to Texas to defend herself. On February 26, 1998, she won in court, and she even became friends with some of the farmers.

FINDING TRUE LOVE

Oprah's fiancé, Stedman Graham Jr., is director of Athletes Against Drugs and president of a public relations firm.

Trusting people in personal relationships has been difficult for Oprah. It is often hard for people who have had a difficult childhood to trust people. It is hard for successful people to trust that others truly like them—not just their wealth and fame.

In 1986, after years of dating and living alone, Oprah met former athlete and marketing consultant Stedman Graham Jr. In an interview with *Ebony* magazine, Oprah described Stedman as "an overwhelmingly decent man." She said, "He has made me realize a lot of the things that were missing in my life, like the sharing that goes on between two people." Oprah and Stedman became engaged in 1992. Fans want the thrill of a fancy wedding, but marriage is still too big a step for Oprah.

THE TRENDSETTER KEEPS GOING...AND GOING

*T*he *Oprah Winfrey Show* still focuses on personal challenges. But after so many other talk show hosts copied her format, Oprah moved on. She set a new trend by adding more positive themes to her show. Even when a show focuses on a particular problem, Oprah looks for ways to help people help themselves—even while she entertains them.

A NEW SPIRIT

In the new show format, when Oprah starts with problems, she ends with solutions. On one show, for example, she interviewed families struggling with "adult children who mooch and won't leave home"—and who expect their parents to pay their bills. Participants talked to a **psychologist** on the air. His message was firm. "Grow up, and take charge of your own life," he said.

MAKING BOOKS POPULAR AGAIN

Oprah, the queen of daytime television, is now telling her fans to read a book instead. She has

Oprah's Book Club

Oprah's choice of books for her club is purely personal, but publishers would love to find ways to influence her. Since 1996, *Oprah's Book Club* has made millionaires of many of the authors it has featured and has earned publishers around $175 million.

Oprah interviews Toni Morrison, author of *Song of Solomon*, in 1996. Interest in the book soared when Oprah selected it for her book club. started a monthly book club that has changed many of her viewers from so-called television couch potatoes to avid readers.

Most books she highlights on the show end up on the *New York Times* best-seller list. A place on this list guarantees success for authors and **publishers.** Her enthusiastic reviews of various books also encourage her viewers to read. To be part of her studio audience, a person must read the suggested book and write about why he or she likes it. As a result of her book club, many publishers and educators think Oprah is one of the best forces for U.S. literacy.

Professor Winfrey's Journey

In many ways, Oprah has become a favorite teacher of many Americans. In addition to teaching values and problem solving on television and other media, she has also taught in the classroom. She taught a graduate-level course in leadership with Stedman at the J. L. Kellogg Graduate School of Management at Northwestern University. Among her guest speakers were former Secretary of State Henry Kissinger and Coretta Scott King, the widow of Dr. Martin Luther King Jr.

As busy and famous as she is, Oprah still finds time for speaking engagements. In a graduation speech at Salem College, a women's college whose students pushed hard to convince her speak there, Oprah said, "I am here because you women will not give up. You wrote me. I got your letters. You e-mailed. You called. I heard you were going to get in a caravan and come to Chicago. You're relentless. You don't know how to take no for an answer… You are my kind of women."

These days, Oprah often describes her life as a spiritual journey. She says, "I'm truly blessed. But I also believe that you tend to create your own blessings. You have to prepare yourself so that when opportunity comes, you're ready. I think that the path of our spiritual involvement is the greatest journey we all take. And I think that is part of the reason why I am as successful as I have been, because success wasn't the goal. I wanted to do good work. I wanted to do well in my life."

In 1999, Oprah was presented with an award by the National Book Foundation for all that her book club has done for authors.

A Typical Day

On most workdays, Oprah wakes up in her 2-story, 24-room Chicago **condominium** between 5 and 6 A.M. From her windows on the 57th floor of Water Tower Place, she has a spectacular view of Lake Michigan. She arrives at Harpo Productions between 6:30 and 7 A.M., unless she decides to join her trainer at 5:30 A.M. for a workout at Harpo's fully-equipped gym.

Oprah spends the next few hours working with her hairdresser and makeup artist to prepare for the two shows she will tape that day. Oprah tapes more than 200 shows a year. While she decides on shoes and

Oprah and Stedman are often on the move between homes. Her ranch may only have a two-car garage, but it also has a helicopter pad!

earrings and has her makeup done, Oprah talks with her **producers** about her "homework." She has studied biographies of her guests, appropriate newspaper clippings, and information about the topics of both shows.

After taping each show, she shakes hands with all 500 members of the audience as they leave. Oprah explains, "It's more memorable than an autograph." During the break between shows, she has lunch, answers letters and phone calls, and changes into a new outfit. Her second taping ends at 2 P.M., at which time she goes to her desk and takes on the job of chairman of her multimillion-dollar corporation. Oprah personally makes all major decisions and signs all the checks.

Oprah can leave as early as 5 P.M., carrying her homework for the next day's shows. However, she often stays as late as 10 P.M. But to which home should Oprah go for dinner? One of her options is to take a helicopter to her 160-acre (65-hectare) farm in nearby Rolling Prairie, Indiana. It has a TV theater, a movie-screening room, a swimming pool, stables for her three thoroughbred horses, and heated kennels for her dogs—including Solomon, her beloved cocker spaniel.

Or, if Oprah and Stedman feel like skiing, they hop into her private jet and zip off to her $3 million mountain ski lodge in Telluride, Colorado. If she wants to see the ocean, she jets to her apartment on Miami's Fisher's Island. Wherever she lands, Oprah says she likes "coming home, kicking off my downtown clothes, filling that tub with one whole bottle of bubble bath, soaking a good long while, then just putting on my old flowered jammies and a pair of fat socks." On weeknights, Oprah usually reads her homework from 10 P.M. until midnight.

Unbeatable Oprah

By the time she was 46, Oprah was being paid at least $70 million a year for *The Oprah Winfrey Show.* However, she had no intention of sitting back to relax. In addition to her show, she has a deal to make six *Oprah Winfrey Presents* films for ABC.

Kick-starting the millennium

Oprah started the new century with a bang. She introduced her own magazine, *O,* in the spring of 2000. The magazine promotes spirituality,

Oprah launches *O* magazine in April 2000. She says: "What I like about 'O' is that it is simple and direct, and it is what a lot of my friends call me."

community, work, and family. She is also challenging her audience to become computer literate.

Oprah has also teamed up with Geraldine Laybourne of cable television's *Nickelodeon* and the Carsey-Werner-Mandabach **production company** to launch a cable television and Internet company called *Oxygen*. *Oxygen* is designed for women and teenagers and is expected to reach up to seven million viewers. To promote it, Oprah hosts shows about the Internet. Oprah hopes this will bring women to the World Wide Web in the same way that her book club brought them into bookstores.

KNOWING WHAT TO SAY AND WHEN

Some wonder if Oprah has some dark secrets she is keeping from the public. She wrote her autobiography and promoted it at the American Booksellers Association Convention in May 1993. But then she withdrew it from publication because, she said, "It didn't have any message. It didn't offer any hope about tomorrow." Today, Oprah is sure she made the right choice. She maintains, "I was still in the heart of the learning curve…. Even in the past year I've learned things about myself that I'm glad I didn't write in an autobiography."

Building on the Positive

How did Oprah become so successful? She did not come from a perfect family. She was not born with wealth, nor with the kind of looks that often unlock the doors of opportunity for women in television. Instead, Oprah was born with wit, intelligence, talent, and an amazing ability to just be herself. No matter who her audience is, Oprah still appears to be natural and open. Best of all, she can get away with saying what other people would like to say themselves, if only they dared. Well-spoken and warm, she shows that she cares about people even when she is being blunt with them.

She has been called "girlfriend to the world" because that is usually how she comes across to the rich and famous and ordinary people alike. After Sarah Ferguson, the Duchess of York, appeared on her show, Oprah sympathized with her, telling her audience: "I would have been kicked out of the palace, too."

> "Now, when I first started out, I was in the, you know, 'fat-black-woman' box, and nobody could figure out how in the world I had gotten to Chicago being not thin, not blond, not white, nothing that fit the mold of what a talk show host or hostess was…"
>
> Oprah Winfrey, 1997

In some ways, Oprah can do no wrong. When she makes mistakes, her fans like to say, "She's only human. She's just like the rest of us." When she is successful, her admirers think, "Oprah is showing me how I can succeed, too." Often funny and frequently wise, when Oprah speaks, people listen.

In October 1994, at the age of 40, Oprah ran in the 26.2-mile (42-kilometer) Marine Corps Marathon in Washington, D.C.

KEY TO SUCCESS

Oprah believes that the key to success is to be prepared for opportunities. She says, "Doing your best in this moment puts you in the best place for the next moment."

Online and in print

Oprah's experience has certainly paid off. Her website has links called *The Show, Your Spirit,* and *Living Smart,* as well as links to other sites such as *Oprah's Book Club* and her *Online Community.* In addition, there are dozens of other websites about her. Any book that Oprah promotes becomes an instant best-seller. Any diet or exercise program she tries becomes the latest fitness trend. She also is chairperson of the Harpo Entertainment Group. Many people think the company is named after Harpo Marx, a famous comedian—until they realize that it is "Oprah" spelled backwards!

> An insider at Harpo Entertainment Group explains Oprah's power: "She owns the show; she owns the **production company**; she owns the studio; and now she owns a major part of the distributor."

Oprah is also a talented actress. In 1998, she starred as Sethe in *Beloved,* which was based on a book by Toni Morrison. In both this film and *The Color Purple,* Oprah played African-American women with the courage to overcome terrible difficulties.

> "The more positive you are about your life, the more positive it will be. The more you complain, the more miserable you will be."
> Oprah Winfrey, 1997

Oprah, shown here with co-star Danny Glover, played the role of a woman who escaped slavery in the film *Beloved*.

HELP FROM WITHOUT AND WITHIN

Oprah reminds her public, "You can't do it all yourself. Don't be afraid to rely on others to help you accomplish your goals." She praises her staff frequently, often rewarding them with expensive gifts. More than anything, Oprah believes that a positive attitude is the key to success. She also advises that it is important to listen to your heart.

THE CHANGING VIEW OF OPRAH WINFREY

Oprah takes center stage on *The Oprah Winfrey Show*. Some members of the staff have found it difficult to work with the new, "positive" format of Oprah's television show.

Oprah has been criticized for using serious topics as a form of entertainment. Has she been too quick to use problems to attract viewers? By the mid–1990s, many people had grown tired of reporters digging up dirt, or looking for embarrassing gossip, about people. Some called this "feeding frenzy journalism."

Over the years, some guests have complained that Oprah misled them. For example, in 1987 the widows of the astronauts of the **Challenger** disaster thought they had been invited on the show to talk about their project, the Challenger Center. They saw it as a way to turn their tragedy into something positive. Instead, Oprah asked the women personal questions about their grief, and this upset them. Oprah decided to change. In 1994, she began

to focus on self-improvement issues, pledging to abandon depressing topics. Her **ratings** took a temporary dip, but Oprah did not give up.

Gradually, the show's ratings climbed back. Oprah apologized for her past efforts to air the public's dirty laundry for entertainment. She said, "I've been guilty of doing trash TV and not even thinking it was trash. I don't want to do it any more. But for the past four years we've been leading the way for doing issues that change people's lives..."

While 1994 marked a positive turn for Oprah's show on the air, it was different behind the scenes. That year, two of her most trusted employees left the show: one she fired, the other resigned. The first, Debra DiMaio, who got Oprah her start in Chicago television, had been making life difficult for Oprah's staff. Ever loyal to her staff, Oprah gave DiMaio several million dollars and asked her to leave.

All Harpo employees are required to sign a secrecy pledge as part of their contracts. When Oprah's publicist resigned later that year, complaining about having to continually cover up for "the disorganized management of Harpo," Oprah refused to give her **severance pay.** At least ten **producers** left the show over the next two years.

Blazing a trail

Oprah is a good example of how a person can make the best use of what life has to offer. More than that, she is blazing a trail for women—especially for African-American women. Oprah is showing them how much they can accomplish if their talents and hard work are matched by equal opportunities in the workplace and in education.

"This woman will be remembered, not in stone wreaths, but by the lives which have grown out of her life, the lives which have been sustained by her life, by the love she gives."
Dr. Maya Angelou, introducing Oprah as guest speaker at Salem College, May 2000

Oprah continues to break new ground. She was in the first generation of African-American women to go to integrated **public schools** and to go to college in large numbers. She was one of the first African-American women to be a television **newscaster**—in fact, she was the first African-American newscaster in Nashville, Tennessee. Clearly, Oprah had very few **role models** for what African-American women could achieve. Lacking many role models, she later became one for others.

In the world of television, today's success is soon old news. Oprah must always keep one step ahead of her competition. What if she should fail? Many say that because she has achieved so much that it would be hard to fault Oprah now. Besides, Oprah always sees failures as learning opportunities. She counts all her blessings—her successes, her friends, and even all the difficult lessons she has learned during her life.

Oprah's journey from poverty to wealth, fame, and success continues to give hope and inspiration to her fans. She knows who she is and what she is supposed to do with her life. "I'm a truth seeker," she says. "That's what I do every day on the show—put out the truth. Some people don't like it, they call it sensational, but I say life is sensational."

Oprah holds her British Academy of Film and Television Arts award in 1994. That year, The Oprah Winfrey Show was voted best foreign program in the U.K.

Oprah Winfrey—Timeline

1954   Oprah Winfrey born on January 29 in Kosciusko, Mississippi

1960   Leaves grandparents' farm to live with mother in Milwaukee, Wisconsin

1963   Lives with father and stepmother in Nashville for one year

1964   Returns to mother in Milwaukee

1966   Attends Lincoln High School in Milwaukee

1968   Attends all-white Nicolet High School in a rich suburb of Milwaukee. Returns to father and stepmother; enrolls in East Nashville High School.

1970   Attends President M. Nixon's White House Conference on Youth

1971   Represents East Nashville High in Outstanding Teenager of America contest. Wins first place in National Forensic League Tournament in Tennessee; goes on to national competition in Palo Alto, California. Gets her first media job reporting for WVOL radio in Nashville. Begins studies in speech and performing arts at Tennessee State University.

1972   Wins Miss Black Nashville, goes on to win Miss Black Tennessee

1973   Moves to television as Nashville's first African-American **news anchor** at WTVF-TV

1976   Moves to Baltimore for job as co-anchor of 6 P.M. news. Asked to co-host local *People Are Talking,* WJZ-TV.

1984   Begins hosting *AM Chicago,* and takes it to number one in the **ratings** within one month. Within the year, show is renamed *The Oprah Winfrey Show* and expanded to a full hour.

1985   Plays Sofia in Alice Walker's *The Color Purple.* Receives nominations for Golden Globe Award and Academy Award for Best Supporting Actress.

1986	*The Oprah Winfrey Show* becomes number one talk show in the United States. Plays Mrs. Thomas in the movie *Native Son*.
1987	Completes her studies and graduates from Tennessee State University
1988	Receives both the People's Choice Award and the International Radio and Television Society's award as Broadcaster of the Year
1992	Becomes engaged to Stedman Graham Jr.
1993	Writes her autobiography, but withdraws it from publication. *Forbes* magazine lists Oprah Winfrey first in its list of "The 40 Top-Earning Entertainers"; Oprah's worth estimated, at that time, around $240 million.
1994	Pledges to refocus her show on uplifting and meaningful subjects
1996	Receives the George Foster Peabody Individual Achievement Award and the International Radio and Television Society's Gold Medal Award
1998	Named one of the 100 Most Influential People of the 20th Century by *Time* magazine. Receives National Academy of Television Arts and Sciences' Lifetime Achievement Award.
1999	Presented with the National Book Foundation's 50th anniversary Gold Medal for what her *Oprah's Book Club* has done for authors, books, and reading. Oprah's net worth is estimated at $750 million; she is paid $70 million a year to do her show.
2000	Launches her interactive cable-TV/Internet website, Oxygen, and her monthly magazine, *O*

GLOSSARY

alma mater school or college a person attended

binge eating eating a large amount of food in a short period of time

Black Pride movement begun during the late 1960s by African-Americans to promote pride in their culture and history

boycott organized refusal to buy or use a particular product or service

Challenger U.S. space shuttle that exploded upon launch in 1986, killing all seven crew members

civil rights rights guaranteed to all U.S. citizens by the Constitution, including the right to vote and the right to equal treatment

condominium apartment or home that is part of an association of neighbors

corncob doll homemade doll made from the dried cob of an ear of corn

curfew time by which a person, especially a teenager, must be off the streets

dashiki long, loose shirt with bold patterns and colors

honors student person who takes a special course of study designed for advanced students

housing project government housing provided at a low cost to the people who live there

integration bringing different ethnic groups into free and equal association

journalist person who works as a news reporter or editor for a newspaper, magazine, or news show

mad cow disease deadly disease of cattle, also called *bovine spongiform encephalopathy* (BSE)

network to make connections with people who can be helpful to you

news anchor main announcer on a news program

newscaster person who reports the news on a public broadcast

Oscar award given each year by the Academy of Motion Picture Arts and Sciences

pioneer person who blazes a trail for others in a chosen path or profession

producer person who supervises the making of a movie, play, radio show, or television show

production company company that makes television shows or movies

psychologist person who studies human minds and behavior

publisher person or company that produces and sells books and other printed material

ratings measure of how many people are watching a show at a given time. TV stations use ratings to sell advertising time. The more popular the show, the more it costs to advertise during its time slot.

role model person who inspires others by his or her example in a profession or way of life

rural having to do with the country, rather than the city

scholarship money given to a student to help pay for education

segregation enforced separation of one group from the rest of society

severance pay money given to a person who has been fired by the company that fired him or her

slave someone who is forced to work for another without pay

sophomore year second year of college

stereotype common and usually over-simplified belief about a group of people

sue to take someone to court to settle a dispute

token person hired not necessarily because of their skills but to show that a place of business is racially integrated

transcend to overcome or rise above limits

volatile explosive and unpredictable

More Books to Read

Nicholson, Lois P. *Oprah Winfrey: Entertainer.* Broomall, Penn.: Chelsea House Publishers, 1997.

Otfinoski, Steven. *Oprah Winfrey: Television Star.* Woodbridge, Conn.: Blackbirch Press, Inc., 1993.

Presnall, Judith J. *Oprah Winfrey.* San Diego, Calif.: Lucent Books, 1998.

Woods, Geraldine. *Oprah Winfrey Story.* Parsippany, N.J.: Silver Burdett Press, 1991.

INDEX